HEALTHY HABITS

ROSIE McCORMICK

First published in the UK in 2002 by

Chrysalis Children's Books
An imprint of Chrysalis Books Group Plc
The Chrysalis Building, Bramley Road, London W10 6SP

Paperback edition first published in 2004

Copyright © Chrysalis Books Group Plc 2002
Text by Rosie McCormick

Editor: Veronica Ross
Designer: Peter Clayman
Illustrator: Woody
Consultant: Kathleen Robertson

ISBN 1 84138 429 1 (hb)
ISBN 1 84138 794 0 (pb)

British Library Cataloguing in Publication Data for this
book is available from the British Library.

Printed In China

Some of the more unfamiliar words used in this book
are explained in the glossary on pages 46 and 47.

CONTENTS

Dear Reader 4

Introduction 5

All about you 6
Eat up! 8
Healthy habits 10
Starting to grow up 12
Feelings and emotions 14
Bugs and bacteria 16
Cigarettes, drugs and alcohol 18

Quiz time 20

Story: Josh's big day 22

Healthy heroes 38

Healthy activities 40

That's astonishing 42

Asking for help 45

Glossary 46

Index 48

Dear Reader

I'm going to let you in on a little secret. You need this book. No, honestly, you really do. You see this book will help you figure out a whole heap of things about growing up, body changes, mood swings and how not to smell. There's important information about smoking and drugs. Also, once you have read these pages you will know just what to say to the adults in your life who nag you about...

Sleep

Food

Your hair

'You had chips yesterday.'

'Who did that to your hair? Give me their name and address and I'll have them arrested!'

'It's not normal to sleep so much. Wake up, I want to take you to see a doctor.'

Attitude

Hygiene

'Pheeewweeeee! Have you been swimming in the village pond or do you need a shower?'

(Boys, this is really aimed at you as girls tend not to be so smelly!)

'Change it or else.'

There's also a great story, astonishing facts, fun activities and rib-tickling jokes. So, now that you know why you need this book so much, it's probably time to read it.

INTRODUCTION

Round about now, life starts to become a little more complicated than it used to be. This, you may be surprised to hear, is partly your fault. All of a sudden, you want to be involved when it comes to making decisions. And, you are beginning to take on some of the responsibility for your health and wellbeing.

Now, the more knowledge you have about something, the more you are able to understand it. For example, if you find yourself looking at your body and saying, 'eeek, why does it look like this?' Then make a point of finding out as much as you can about it. This book is a good starting point.

And, if you sometimes feel a bit fed up and feel that your friends and family just don't understand you, then read on. (If you need to know more, there is a list of useful phone numbers and websites on page 45.)

ALL ABOUT YOU

Okay, let's find out a bit more about you, your body and how clean and healthy you think you are... In fact, while we are at it let's examine your teeth, hair and nails. After all, we don't want to miss anything!

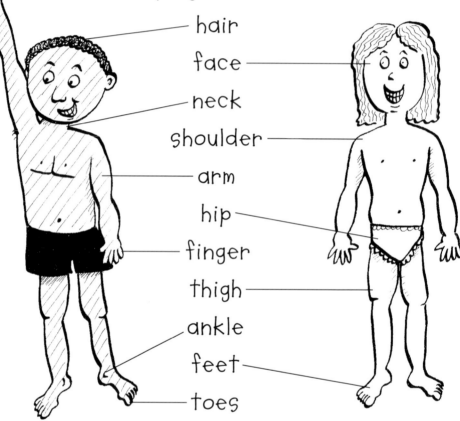

hair

face

neck

shoulder

arm

hip

finger

thigh

ankle

feet

toes

BODY BEAUTIFUL

Your body is a complicated machine with a number of systems designed to do a particular job. If you want your body to keep on working well, then you need to look after it. With luck, you will be using your body for a long time, so it makes sense to put in a little effort to keep it ticking over nicely.

complex fab body

AND ONE, AND TWO...

Exercise is a must, even if it's just for 15 minutes each day. Exercise gives you more energy, your lungs work better, your bones and muscles become stronger. It reduces stress and helps you to sleep – so make sure you do some.

'Not you again, Stanley.'

'Er, I thought it looked like it might rain!'

NIGHT, NIGHT!

You need at least eight hours sleep each night. Your body grows, repairs and strengthens itself while you are sleeping so don't stay up all night watching TV or playing computer games! (On the other hand, don't lie in bed all day either!)

FOOD GLORIOUS FOOD

Food gives us the energy we need to play, work and study. A good diet will help keep you active and healthy.

ALL WASHED UP

It's really important to keep clean. Dirt on the skin attracts bacteria which can cause disease. So, wash every day and don't forget to clean your teeth!

What do you call someone who never blows his nose?
Ronnie

EAT UP!

Now you've heard the saying 'you are what you eat' (does a mental picture of a person with a pizza head, burger body and chip legs suddenly spring to mind? Well don't worry if it does because the following information will help you change all that!) In order to keep every part of your body (both inside and out) fit and healthy you need to eat, yes, a healthy balanced diet. And here's how to do it.

'Oh mum, not burger and chips for tea! I wanted avocado, mozzarella and tomato on a bed of lettuce with a dribble of virgin olive oil!'

Nurse, I need to see a doctor.
Which doctor?
No, an ordinary one will do!

ESSENTIAL FOODS

Only a healthy balanced diet will help your body stay fit and strong. That's why it's important to make sure that the foods you eat contain minerals – especially iron – vitamins, protein, carbohydrates, fibre and fats. And in order to keep your energy levels high, always try to eat breakfast and never skip meals. And yes, another nag – try to eat five pieces of fruit or veg each day.

FOOD WATCH

Red meat, especially liver, and leafy green vegetables, such as broccoli and spinach, are rich in iron. Iron helps to carry oxygen around the body.

Fish, wholemeal bread, eggs, fruit and cereals contain vitamins. Your body needs vitamins to keep your bones, teeth and eyes in tip-top shape.

Eggs, milk, cheese and nuts provide you with protein to build your muscles, bones and teeth.

Starchy carbohydrates, such as potatoes, pasta, rice and bread, keep you warm and give you energy.

Cereal and wholemeal grain are full of fibre. Fibre helps you to digest the food you eat.

Vegetable oils, nuts and fish are full of fats and oils. They transport vitamins around your body.

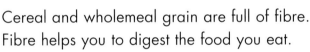
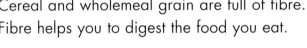

DRINK UP

Two-thirds of your body is made up of water. But, you lose water through your skin (especially when you sweat) and when you go to the toilet. To replace the lost fluid and keep your body working properly you need to drink at least eight glasses of water each day.

Healthy Habits

Now it may take up a little of your time, but being clean and generally unsmelly is an important part of staying healthy. If you don't wash, various parts of your body start to become oily and dirty. Eeeek! And if you don't brush your teeth your breath starts to smell – need I say more. So, here are some tips on what to do and how to do it!

Terrific Teeth

It's important to brush your teeth at least twice a day. In the morning and evening is best. If you do this you will keep your teeth and gums healthy and strong. But if you don't, tiny bits of food will collect in your mouth and harm your teeth and gums. Your breath will smell as well.

Your teeth are covered by enamel – the hardest material in your body. That's just as well as they have to grind and chew and chomp for many years.

TEETH PATROL
1. Brush at least twice a day.
2. Don't have too many sweets and fizzy drinks.
3. Have regular check-ups at the dentist.
4. Change your toothbrush regularly.

10

LONG NAILS

Fingernails are made from keratin, the same material that your hair is made from. Nails grow quickly. It takes about six months for a nail to grow from the cuticle to the tip. Always remember to scrub your nails to remove any dirt.

Doctor, doctor. My hair is falling out. What can I do? Here, put it in this paper bag.

SKIN HYGIENE

It's important to keep your skin clean. The only way you can do this is to wash regularly. (Are you listening boys, I said regularly!) This is because bacteria grow quickly on dirty, sweaty skin. And if you don't wash you start to pong. Phewwww!

HAPPENING HAIR

We have hair to help keep us warm and protect our skin. Your hair grows about 1mm every three to four days and you probably have about 100,000 hairs on your head. Have you ever wondered why you don't feel anything when you get your hair cut? Well that's because only the base of the hair, where the hair grows, is alive. The hair above the surface is dead.

Wash your hair every few days to keep it healthy and clean.

11

STARTING TO GROW UP

You'll know when you hit puberty – or rather when puberty hits you – because you won't know yourself and your parents will have their doubts about who you are too! You see, the thing about puberty is that it's a time of many changes. The body that's good at climbing trees and hanging upside down from high, dangerous places starts to do odd things.

PUBERTY FOR BOYS

For boys it often begins when their voices begin to sound a bit croaky. Then at the worst moments they make high pitched squeaking sounds. This happens because the male voice box starts to get bigger and a more adult sounding voice develops.

Between the ages of about 10–14, your body starts to change and you begin to look more like an adult. It is the time when your body gets ready for having children. This is called puberty.

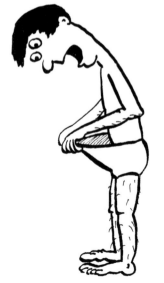

OH NO, I'M ALL HAIRY!

There's more. Hair begins to grow all over the place. Under your arms, on your legs, chest and arms, face – and yes – around your privates. This hair is called pubic hair. (So, you are turning into a hairy, squeaking creature, got it so far?) While this is happening you will start to grow taller and broader. Your penis and testicles will get bigger, as will your feet and hands. Oh, and you might become a little spotty.

WHY ME?

Why on earth is this happening? I can hear you asking. Well you can pin the blame on hormones which are released by a gland in the brain called the pituitary gland. For boys, a hormone called testosterone, plays a big part in their physical development. But hormones don't just cause physical changes they can affect your feelings and emotions too.

pituitary gland

Doctor, doctor, all my friends think I'm a liar. **I find that hard to believe!**

PUBERTY FOR GIRLS

Girls experience some of the same things. They grow taller, sometimes broader, their feet and hands get bigger. Hair grows under their arms and on their arms and legs, pubic hair grows, female reproductive parts develop, breasts grow, they get spotty and periods start. What fun huh!?

FEELINGS AND EMOTIONS

As you grow older life does seem to become more complicated. From time to time you will find yourself disagreeing with your parents, brothers, sisters, friends – in fact with most of the people in your life! You can feel really angry, or very sad, bored, confused, lonely and misunderstood without really knowing why. And, the things you used to like doing so much, like riding your bike round the park, now seem SOOooo boring. But you can't do the things you want to because you are not old enough.

BUT I DON'T WANT TO DO THAT

You want more space and time to yourself but grown-ups are still insisting that you join in with everything they do. Your parents no longer understand you, or so it seems, and you no longer understand them. You feel pressure at home and pressure at school. In fact, life can seem like one big pressure cooker waiting to explode.

BUT MUM THIS IS A REALLY COOL HAIRSTYLE

As you get older you begin to think a lot about who you are, what you like, what you don't like, where you fit in in the world, what you are good at and the kind of people you enjoy being with. For years your parents or guardians have answered these questions for you. But now you want to take more responsibility for your life. As a result, you have more to say about things and this can lead to disagreements.

Doctor, doctor, I've lost my memory. **My goodness, when did this happen?** When did what happen?

LET'S JUST TALK IT OVER

When this happens, just remember that the people who love you, will always love you. And believe it or not, they do understand what you are going through because they had to grow up too. If you do have a problem, try talking to a friend you trust, or perhaps a teacher you get on well with. And don't forget that mum and dad would hate to think that you were miserable and felt you couldn't tell them. So, let people know what's bothering you.

BUGS AND BACTERIA

One minute you're feeling fine, the next minute you feel as if you've been run over by a truck. That's because, all around you, floating through the air, in water and hiding in the food you eat, are microscopic creatures that can make you feel ill. They are called germs.

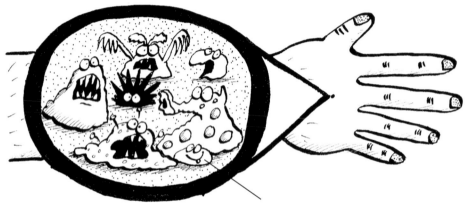

bugs under a microscope

GERM ALERT

Bacteria, viruses and fungi are organisms that we call germs. Bacteria are tiny, living things that are found in the air and earth, on plants and animals and on us. Some bacteria are good for us because they help keep the digestive system healthy and fight off other germs. But others can cause infections.

IT'S YOUR TURN NOW

Viruses need other living cells to survive. Once they find a home, they spread quickly, making you and others ill. Chickenpox and mumps are viruses.

DAMP DEVILS

Fungi are plant-like organisms that feed on plants, food, and animals. They like damp, warm environments. When someone has athlete's foot they have a fungal infection.

FIGHTING BACK

The best way to prevent illnesses caused by germs is by protecting yourself. If you wash your hands often, you will prevent many germs from getting into your body. Another way to fight infections is to be immunised. When you were a baby you were given injections to protect you against dangerous infections. This is called immunisation.

Doctor, doctor, I think I need glasses. You've got that right, this is a video shop.

I'm coming to get you!

Remember to wash your hands:

after you've been to the toilet
after playing with your pets
after you've blown your nose
after touching rubbish or anything dirty
before you eat

INVASION OF THE GERMS!

17

CIGARETTES, DRUGS AND ALCOHOL

Statistics tell us that one third of all young people smoke by the time they are 19 years old. And many try their first cigarette between the ages of 9 and 12. This means that one third of young people don't care if they harm themselves because smoking is really bad for you – and that's a fact.

Why do people smoke?

1. They think it makes them look cool.
2. Their friends do it.
3. Their parents smoke so they give it a try.
4. Older brothers and sisters smoke
5. They are curious.

Wow! That looks really cool!

If you are under 16 years of age, it's illegal to buy cigarettes.

NO SMOKING PLEASE!

Cigarettes and cigarette smoke contain many harmful ingredients, such as tar, carbon monoxide, pesticides and poisonous metals, such as arsenic, and ammonia. They also contain nicotine, a highly addictive and poisonous substance.

WHAT SMOKING DOES TO YOU

Smoking causes lung cancer (experts believe it contributes to other kinds of cancer too). It also causes heart disease, bronchitis and bad blood circulation. And if that isn't enough, it also makes your breath smell, stains your teeth and fingers yellow, makes you smelly, and makes your skin wrinkly.

LUNG DAMAGE

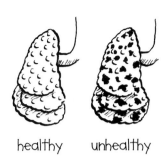

healthy lung   unhealthy lung

When a cigarette is smoked, smoke passes along the bronchial tubes leading to the lungs. These tubes contain tiny hairs that keep germs and dirt out of the lungs. Tobacco damages or destroys these hairs. And, soot and tar stick to the lungs and the bronchial tubes. This can cause coughs and breathing problems.

IT WAS HIM!

The man to blame for the introduction of tobacco into Britain was Sir Walter Raleigh. He brought tobacco leaves back with him after an expedition to North America in the 16th century.

UNDERSTANDING DRUGS AND ALCOHOL

Drugs and alcohol can make you feel all kinds of things, happy, sad, confused, dizzy and tired. They can also make you feel very sick. The chemicals in drugs and alcohol are taken into your bloodstream very quickly, but the effects can last for hours. Like cigarettes, drugs and alcohol can damage your health. So be sensible, respect your body – don't harm it!

QUIZ TIME

Now just to make sure that you've been paying attention here's a little quiz to test your memory.

Teacher:
'Simon, why are taking that snake into the exam?'
Simon:
'It's an adder, sir!'

1 Which of these foods contain protein?
a) potatoes
b) eggs
c) fruit

2 Where is your pituitary gland?
a) in your liver
b) in your brain
c) in your stomach

3 Who introduced tobacco to Britain?
a) Sir Walter Raleigh
b) Sir Francis Drake
c) Napoleon

4 Which of these foods contain iron?
a) red meat and green veg
b) jelly and ice-cream
c) chips

5 What is the main ingredient in your body?
a) water
b) chocolate
c) blood

6 What are skin, hair and nails made of?
a) plastic
b) keratin
c) ivory

7 What helps to make your body change during puberty?
a) burgers and chips
b) designer clothes
c) hormones

8 What are mammary glands?
a) breasts
b) teeth
c) a rock band

9 What is bacteria?
a) a mouthwash
b) a tiny single-celled organism
c) a dessert

10 What is the addictive ingredient in tobacco?
a) carbon dioxide
b) ammonia
c) nicotine

11 What is the hardest material in your body?
a) bone
b) enamel
c) keratin

12 What is athlete's foot?
a) A fungal infection
b) A sore toe
c) A type of trainer

ANSWERS

1 b; 2 b; 3 a; 4 a; 5 a; 6 b; 7 c; 8 a; 9 b; 10 c; 11 b; 12 a

Josh's big day

Josh pulled his hood up over his head and shivered.
A cold North wind was blowing across the Beacon Hill school
sport's field. Josh imagined that an invisible demon was
breathing icy puffs of cold air all over him – just for the fun
of it. The demon had a fixed, thin-lipped grin on his face
and his crystal body was hidden in a swirling cloak of
shimmering cloud.

Josh hunched forward and looked at the sky, his eyes
squinting against the wind. The sky was a silver-grey.
'It'll snow soon,' he thought. 'Thank goodness there's
only 20 more minutes of training.'

As Josh turned to do one more lap of the track, he was
overcome by an attack of coughing. His chest hurt and
through each bout of coughing he struggled to get his
breath. This had been happening to him a lot and
his coach had noticed it too.

'Are you feeling okay,' Mr Kenton, his coach kept asking him. 'You haven't been yourself recently. I hope you're not coming down with something just before the county trials.'

But Josh had reassured him that everything was okay.

Now, once again, Mr Kenton was watching Josh with a look of concern on his face. Josh decided that he'd better get on with that last lap before Mr Kenton had a chance to corner him and nag him again.

Trying to stifle a cough and ignoring the pain in his chest Josh set off at a steady, even pace. At 13 years of age, he was a talented 800 and 1200 metres runner. In fact, he was one of the best in his School – Beacon Hill Comprehensive. Mr Kenton was confident that he would do well in the county trials in two weeks time. And he had hopes that Josh would finish in the top three in the finals. Well, that was until a few weeks ago.

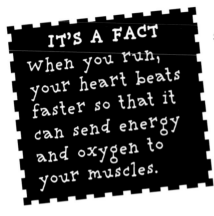

Josh finished his lap in a much slower time than usual and headed for the changing rooms and a hot shower. His legs felt like jelly and his chest was still aching. There was no doubt about it, in the last week or two his body had just not been responding.

Josh stood under the shower for several minutes, letting the hot water soothe his tired limbs. As he did so, he allowed himself to daydream about the trials. As usual, he imagined himself winning and being the school hero. Suddenly his daydreams were interrupted by Mr Kenton's familiar booming voice.

'Where's Josh, I want to talk to him?' shouted Mr Kenton, as he glared at the other boys in the changing room. 'He's just taking a shower,' answered Andy Green.

'Josh, when you're finished in there,' yelled Mr Kenton, 'I want a word.'

Josh didn't reply. He simply turned the shower off, wrapped himself in his towel and padded towards his locker.

Then, as he dried and dressed himself, Mr Kenton stood over him and ranted. He told Josh that he was running like an injured rabbit and acting like a cornered fox. Mr Kenton always painted a clear picture of things. He told Josh that he needed to go and see a doctor. If he didn't he would bring one to see him!

When Josh was certain that Mr Kenton had said all that he wanted to say, he simply zipped up his jacket, grabbed his school bag and walked out of the dressing room without saying a word. Mr Kenton watched him go.

Ten minutes later Josh was in the park opposite his house, leaning against his favourite tree and smoking a cigarette.

After a few drags he began to relax. 'Kenton's such a whiner,' he thought to himself. He's getting his knickers in a twist about nothing.' Josh finished his cigarette and then lit another one. He was completely relaxed now.

IT'S A FACT
Smoking cigarettes is an expensive habit. It will make you poor and the tobacco companies, governments and shops rich.

Josh stood and looked across at his house for ages. Most of the lights were on, it was getting late, past teatime. He was just about to go when he heard a familiar voice calling.

'How's the champ doing today, or is that chump?' the voice said from behind the tree. 'Give us a fag.' It was his brother Patrick.

'Get your own,' replied Josh.

Patrick grabbed Josh playfully and wrestled him to the ground. 'Hey, who gave you your first cigarette? Come on, hand them over,' said Patrick.

Eventually Patrick managed to snatch the cigarette packet from out of Josh's jacket pocket. Patrick handed Josh a cigarette and then took one for himself.

Josh lit both cigarettes
and then the boys stood
together telling each
other about their day.
Patrick was 17 and had
just started working in
a sport's shop. Josh told
him about his training
and Mr Kenton's nagging.

Then, when they had finished smoking, they collected their
things and walked slowly towards home.

'Where have you been Josh? And you Patrick?
Your tea is ruined. You'll have to have beans on toast instead,'
said the boys' mum. Her face was tired and as usual she looked
worried. She was a nurse. For several years now she had been
working a night shift at the local hospital so that she could be at
home during the day.

'I've got to go to work boys.
So you're in charge of the
girls tonight, okay?
Don't go out
anywhere,'
said Mum, as
she grabbed
her coat from
the stand in
the hallway.
Then kissing
both boys on
the cheek,

she shouted a quick goodbye to the eleven-year-old twins who were upstairs in their room listening to music.

'BYE, see you later,' the girls shouted as mum stood in front of the hall mirror and quickly combed her hair.

'Just go to work and don't worry,' said Patrick, opening the front door for her and ushering her out. 'Go on, you'll be late.'

'Did Dad drop off my new trainers,' shouted Josh, as mum made her way down the front path.

'You'll be lucky,' said Patrick sarcastically.

'No he didn't love. Won't the ones you've got do for now?' mum shouted back.

Josh didn't bother to reply. He threw his coat and school bag on the floor in the hallway and slowly walked up the stairs to the bedroom he shared with Patrick.

IT'S A FACT
Scientists think it's possible to become addicted to smoking cigarettes in just a few days. So don't start!

Josh lay on his bed and stared at the ceiling. Patrick and Josh had shared this bedroom forever. The ceiling was still decorated with the glow-in-the-dark stars and planets that their dad had stuck on when Josh was five years old. That was just a few months before he left home for good.

28

On the wall above his bed were posters of some of his favourite track and field athletes. Josh believed that he could be as successful as any one of them. He had the talent, everyone told him so. He just had to get through this difficult time. Josh lay back on his bed and lit a cigarette. His mum didn't  know that he and Patrick smoked. And they rarely smoked in the house in case she smelt it. But Josh needed just one more cigarette. One more to help him forget how badly he was running.

The next two weeks of training were no better. His cough wasn't going away and his lap times were definitely getting worse. And on top of that, Mr Kenton was really freaking Josh out. He had stopped ranting and raving at him. Instead he hardly spoke to Josh at all. Most of the time he focused his attention on some of the other boys, like Andy Green, who was running much better than Josh.

In a way Josh was relieved. He hated being nagged.

IT'S A FACT
Coughing is your body's way of clearing blockages from your throat so that you can breathe properly.

But a part of him didn't like being ignored either. It made him feel out of it, no longer part of the team.

Finally the day of the county trials arrived. On a cold February afternoon, right after lunch, Josh and the other boys boarded the school bus. Mr Kenton did one final head count and then signalled to the driver that they could go. Thirty minutes later they were at Heatherton sports club for an afternoon of track and field competitions against some of the best athletes in the county.

As soon as the boys had changed, they went outside to warm up and prepare themselves for their heats. Andy was up first. He was running in the 400 metres. The boys watched as Andy ran well. His pace was good and they could tell that he had held enough back for a final sprint. Andy won his heat and Mr Kenton beamed.

IT'S A FACT
Most people breathe in and out about 14-16 times a minute. After exercise this rises to more than 60 times a minute!

Josh's 800 metre heat was next. Like Andy, Josh started well. His first 400 metres were better than anything he had done in the last month or so. Josh was really pleased with himself.

Out of the corner of his eye he caught sight of Andy and Mr Kenton cheering him on. Yes, he felt good.

But suddenly, with about 250 metres to go, something began to go wrong. Josh started to cough and he couldn't stop. Then a searing pain ripped through his chest and side and made him stumble. He felt dizzy and his legs just wouldn't work. Before he knew it, he was on the floor in a crumpled heap.

'What's going on?' exclaimed Josh, gasping and reaching for his chest.

Within seconds Mr Kenton and Andy Green were kneeling beside him.

'Are you okay Josh?' said Andy looking concerned.

31

'No, he's not okay. He's far from okay,' replied Mr Kenton between gritted teeth.

'I want you to stand up Josh,' said Mr Kenton. 'I'm going to help you back to the changing room.'

Just as Mr Kenton said this, Josh heard a loud cheer. Glancing over his shoulder he caught sight of Timothy O' Riley crossing the finishing line first. Josh had beaten Tim in every race they had ever run. Josh felt sick inside.

Mr Kenton ordered Josh to take a shower and then relax on the bench in the changing room. He said, his voice still sounding stern, that he would be back shortly.

Fifteen minutes later Mr Kenton returned with a woman Josh had never seen before.

'Josh, this is Dr Marshall. She's the doctor here at the sport's club. I've asked her to take a look at you. Now Josh I want you to be honest. I want you to tell Dr Marshall exactly how you've been feeling, especially today. Will you do that for me?' asked Mr Kenton. Josh simply nodded.

'I'm going out to see how the others are getting on. I'll be back in a while.'

And with that Mr Kenton walked out of the changing room.

Josh sat there in silence waiting to see what was going to happen next. Dr Marshall simply looked at him for a few moments and then finally she spoke.
'Josh, do you smoke?' she asked softly.

Josh just stared at her but remained silent.

'I can smell cigarette smoke on your hair and your fingers are a little yellow. And from what Mr Kenton tells me you've had a bad cough for a while now,' Dr Marshall continued.

'What's that got to do with anything,' snapped Josh.

'Well quite a lot actually. You see I'm guessing that you've had a cold and because you smoke that has allowed a chest infection to set in. I'll listen to your chest in a minute just to be sure. Tobacco smoke damages the bronchial tubes in your lungs. They become blocked and cannot keep germs out. So infections get in and make you ill. And if you are smoking the chances are you're not eating properly.

IT'S A FACT
Your lungs are organs specially designed for breathing. You have two lungs. They are inside your chest behind your ribcage.

Your body just can't cope, she said.

'I can cope,' snapped Josh.

'Josh, why do you smoke?' continued Dr Marshall.

'It makes me feel calm, relaxes me,' said Josh.
'I feel like I'm under a lot of pressure, especially
with my running.'

'I do understand Josh. But smoking doesn't really help.
If anything it makes things worse. Josh you are an athlete.
Athletes cannot smoke. As you discovered today smoking
affects breathing, stamina and overall performance.
You have to stop,' said Dr Marshall.

'I don't believe you,' said Josh angrily. My dad has
smoked for 20 years and he's okay! My brother Patrick
smokes, most of my mates smoke, in fact loads of people
I know smoke. They all seem fine to me!'

'I can guarantee you that eventually their health will be
affected. But we're talking about you Josh, not your dad
or your friends. You've just messed up a big opportunity.
Mr Kenton told me just before I came in here that you
are one of the most talented athletes he's ever seen.

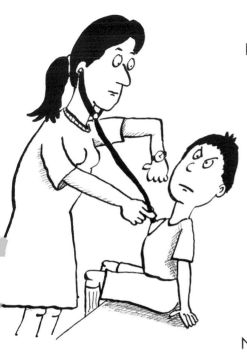

But he can see you throwing it all away just because you smoke,' continued Dr Marshall.

'Mr Kenton knows I smoke,' said Josh with a surprised look on his face. 'But he's never said anything to me.'

'Of course he knows you smoke. He's not stupid. Now let me listen to your chest.'

Josh sat there in silence while Dr Marshall examined him. 'Well you've got a very nasty infection. You are going to need a course of antibiotics to clear that up,' said Dr Marshall with a heavy sigh. 'I'll write you out a prescription and I'll send a note to your GP.'

Just then Mr Kenton came in. He had just watched two of Josh's team mates win the javelin and hurdles trials.

'Well, we've had a long chat,' said Dr Marshall. 'Josh knows the score. He understands that if he carries on smoking cigarettes he might as well stop running now.'

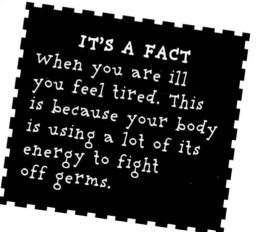

IT'S A FACT
When you are ill you feel tired. This is because your body is using a lot of its energy to fight off germs.

Aware that Mr Kenton was just standing there staring at him, Josh felt like crawling into a corner and hiding. He knew that he had let everyone down badly.

'I'm sorry. I didn't know that smoking was that bad', said Josh. 'And now I've really blown it. I've messed up big time.'

'If you stop now and give your body a chance to recover, you will be back on form in a few months time. You still have a chance Josh. But you have to deal with it right away,' said Mr Kenton, as he sat down beside Josh.

IT'S A FACT
Smokers are more likely than non-smokers to have serious diseases.

'How come you let me run? I've been rubbish for ages,' asked Josh.

'I had a feeling this would happen,' said Mr Kenton. 'I figured that this might be the only way to get through to you.

Nothing else was working, was it?' said Mr Kenton
with a smile.

'You know my mum was really excited about today,'
said Josh as he buried his face in his hands. 'I've let
her down too. I'll try to stop smoking cigarettes.
I think I can do it. It's just that I seem to need them.'

'You feel that way because you've become addicted
to nicotine, Josh. But you're tough. I know you can get
through this,' said Mr Kenton, putting an arm around Josh.
'Now let's go out there and cheer on those team mates
of yours. After all you'll want their support when
you're leading the field again in a few months time.'

Josh stood up and Mr Kenton placed an arm around his
shoulder. Then together they walked out of the changing room.

Healthy Heroes

Louis Pasteur
1822–1895

For centuries doctors had been unable to discover how diseases were caused. But a French chemist called Louis Pasteur was to change all that. He realized that there were germs in the air that made people ill.

He made this discovery when he realized that germs could turn wine sour. So he experimented by boiling the wine and then cooling it down. This killed the germs. He called this process pasteurisation. This method is still used today; most dairy products are pasteurised.

Pasteur went on to use his discovery to help fight diseases. He examined the blood of healthy people and compared it with the blood of people with diseases. He discovered that when people were infected with disease their blood contained germs. Pasteur went on to develop vaccinations for chickenpox, cholera, diphtheria, anthrax and rabies.

JOSEPH LISTEUR
1827–1912

In the 19th century, many people who had operations died afterwards from an infection. Joseph Lister, a Professor of Surgery at Glasgow University, was determined to do something about this. Louis Pasteur's discovery of germs in the air helped him solve the problem. Lister understood that open wounds needed to be protected from germs. So, he experimented on an 11-year-old boy, who had been run over by a cart and had fractured his leg. He cleaned the wound and placed a dressing covered with carbolic acid over it. Lister hoped that the carbolic acid would kill any germs in the wound. It worked. And the boy survived.

Lister went on to develop a carbolic spray which could be used to spray the operating area. As well as this, Lister made sure that his operating theatre was kept clean, that all surgeons wore clean clothes, and that instruments were disinfected. Lister's methods were adopted by doctors all over the world and the lives of thousands of patients were saved. Thank goodness!

HEALTHY ACTIVITIES

Dear Reader
The following experiments are designed to help you find out about your body and how it works. Record the results in a a notebook and don't be afraid to repeat an experiment if the results aren't quite what you expected.

TOUCHY FEELY

To find out just how amazing your skin is challenge a friend to put on a blindfold. Then ask her to use her fingers to examine a number of objects. Her skin will let her know if the things she is touching are hot, cold, rough, smooth, wet or dry, and so on. And her skin will help her to identify the objects too.

Is it an apple?

TONGUE TIED

Your tongue is one of the body's most mobile muscles and helps to shape the sounds of speech. To find out just how important your tongue is for speaking, hold the tip of your tongue and try to say something. Can you speak clearly? I bet you can't.

40

Hey, good looking

Look in a mirror and watch your eyebrows. They change position according to your mood and facial expression. Try smiling, frowning and looking surprised. Watch what your eyebrows do.

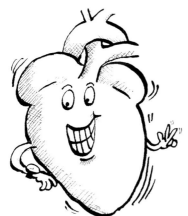

Heart Beat

Your blood is pumped around your body by your heart. You can work out how many times per minute your heart beats by checking your pulse. First place two fingers on your wrist. Then wait until your feel the first beat. Look at a watch and count how many beats you feel in one minute.

Finger Fact

Did you know that your fingerprints are unique? No two people in the whole world have exactly the same prints. Get an ink pad and some clean white paper. Then compare your prints to your friends' prints. There are five basic print types.

⭐ **SNEEZY WHEEZY**
On average, most children catch up to eight colds a year with each cold lasting 5 to 7 days.

aaachooo

YUK!

⭐ **SKIN DEEP**
Your skin is the largest organ in your body. It weighs about as much as four bags of sugar. But did you know that you are constantly losing it – your skin that is? You will have shed about 18kgs of skin by the time you are 75 years old! In fact, most household dust is made up of dead skin cells.

⭐ **FOOD FOR THOUGHT**
If you eat a healthy breakfast, such as cereal with milk and some whole grain toast, you will do better at school. A healthy diet gives you energy and helps your brain to function well.

⭐ **EVERY BREATH YOU TAKE**
In just one day, you breathe about 15,000 litres of air.

THAT HURT!

Thousands of years ago, people used sharpened shells, flint and shark's teeth to shave their hair.

A RIPE OLD AGE

Today, people in many parts of the world live twice as long as their ancestors did. In Europe 500 years ago, people lived to be about 40 years of age. Now it is almost 80 years. This is because people have a much better diet, they are cleaner, and they have all kinds of medicines and vaccinations to fight off illness.

GROWING PAINS

Some children have growing pains between the ages of 3 and 5 years, and 8 and 12 years. Growing pains usually occur in your legs. So, if you've been getting these pains, don't worry your legs aren't about to fall off, you're just getting taller.

SAY CHEESE

When you smile, 30 muscles work together so that you can produce a nice, cheesy grin.

YOU'VE GROWN!

When you lie down you become taller. That's because when you are standing your spine squashes up a bit, making you about 1cm shorter.

⭐ **STAND CLEAR** When you cough you can expel air at up to 100km/h. And when you sneeze air can travel as fast as 160km/h.

⭐ **SWEET DREAMS** You might not remember your dreams, but you dream for about one-quarter of the time you are asleep.

⭐ **WHERE DID THEY GO?** On average you lose about 50 hairs from your head each day.

So lazy

⭐ **ZZzzzzzzz** By the time you reach 60, you will have slept away almost 20 years.

⭐ **I CAN'T BREATHE!** Long ago, people believed that if you were ill, your soul could leave your body through your nose. So they blocked up a sick person's nose until they were well again.

Asking for Help

H ere are telephone numbers and web site addresses for organizations that offer help, advice and information to young people and parents on the subjects that have been discussed in this book.

Cancer Information Service 0800 783 3339
Careline 020 8514 5444
Child Call 0800 774 466
Child Helpline 0800 919 300
ChildcareLink 0800 096 0296
Childline 0800 1111
Childline Bullying Line (Scotland only) 0800 441111
Drinkline 0800 917 8282
Drugs in Schools Helpline 0808 8000 800
Epilepsy 0808 800 5050
Kidscape 020 7730 3300
National AIDS Helpline 0800 567 123
National Association for Children of Alcoholics 0800 358 3456
National Drugs Helpline 0800 77 66 00
NSPCC Child Protection Helpline 0800 800 5000
Skill – National Bureau for Students with Disabilities 0800 328 5050
TALKadoption 0808 808 1234

On Line
Drug Education and Awareness for Life at www.deal.org
Teen Advice Online at www.teenadviceonline.org
Teens Helping Teens at www.ldteens.org
(this is by and for dyslexic children)

ANTIBIOTICS Chemical substances that can fight germs. Penicillin is an antibiotic.

BACTERIA Types of germ. Bacteria can make you ill.

BAD BLOOD CIRCULATION When the flow of blood from the heart to the arteries and veins is not as efficient as it should be.

BRONCHITUS An infection of the bronchial tubes. If someone has bronchitus they usually have a bad cough.

CARBOLIC ACID An antiseptic or disinfectant.

CELLS The smallest units of living matter that make up each bit of your body.

DIGESTIVE SYSTEM The part of the body that is responsible for breaking down food so that it can be absorbed and used.

DISINFECT The process of destroying germs.

GLANDS Parts of your body that produce liquids (such as sweat and saliva) that the body can use.

HEART DISEASE An illness that affects the health and function of the heart.

HORMONES Chemicals that tell parts of your body when and how to work.

INFECTION You have an infection when germs invade your body and make you feel unwell.

KERATIN A protein that is found in the outer layers of hair, skin and nails.

LUNG CANCER A disease that damages the lungs so that they cannot function properly.

LUNGS Sponge-like organs in your body that enable you to breathe.

MICROSCOPIC Not large enough to be seen by the human eye.

MUSCLES Bundles of tissues in the body that can be tightened or loosened to make the body move.

ORGANISM A living thing.

OXYGEN A gas found in air. All living things need to breathe oxygen to stay alive.

PENIS The male sex organ. It is also the delivery pipe for urine.

PERIODS Blood that passes out of a woman's body each month.

PESTICIDES Chemicals, usually sprayed on crops, that kill insects and rodents.

PUBIC HAIR Hair that grows between your legs.

PULSE The beating of the arteries caused by blood being pumped through them by the heart.

REPRODUCTIVE PARTS The parts of the body that are used to create a baby.

TESTICLES Male reproductive glands. They make and store a man's sperm supply.

STRESSED To be worried and unhappy about something.

VIRUSES Types of germ. Chickenpox is a virus.

VOICE BOX Another term for the larynx. A hollow organ which is made up of an air passage to the lungs. It also contains the vocal cords.

INDEX

alcohol 19
ammonia 18
anthrax 38
arsenic 18
athlete's foot 17

bacteria 7, 11, 16, 46
blood 18, 38, 41, 46
body hair 12
body parts 6
bones 7, 9
bread 9
breasts 13
bronchial tubes 19
bronchitus 18, 46

carbohydrates 8, 9
carbolic acid 39, 46
carbon monoxide 18
cells 16, 46
cereal 9, 42
cheese 9
chickenpox 16, 38
cholera 38
cigarettes 18, 19, 22–37
colds 42
coughs 19, 44

diet 7, 8, 42
digestive system 16, 46
diptheria 38
disease 7, 38
drugs 19

eggs 9
enamel 10
energy 8, 9
exercise 7
'eyebrows' activity 41

fats 8
feelings and emotions
   14–15
'fingerprint' activity 41
fish 9
fibre 8, 9
food 7, 8–9, 42

fruit 8, 9
fungi 16, 17

germs 16, 17, 19,
   38, 39
growing pains 43
growing up 12, 13

hair 11, 43, 44
'heart' activity 41
heart disease 18, 46
helplines 45
hormones 13, 46

immunisation 17
infections 16, 46
iron 8, 9

keeping clean 7, 10, 11,
   17
keratin 11, 46

Lister, Joseph 39
liver 9
lung cancer 18, 47
lungs 7, 18, 19, 47

mammals 13
mammary glands 13
meat 9
milk 9, 42
minerals 8
mumps 16
muscles 7, 9, 43, 47

nails 11
nicotine 18
nuts 9

organisms 16, 17, 47
oxygen 9, 47

parents 12, 14, 15
pasta 9
Pasteur, Louis 38
pasteurization 39
penis 12, 47

pesticides 18
pituitary gland 13
potatoes 9
protein 8
puberty 12, 13
pubic hair 12, 13, 47

rabies 38
Raleigh, Sir Walter 19
rice 9

skin 11, 42
sleep 7, 44
smoking 18, 19, 22–37
spots 12, 13
stress 7

tar 18
teeth 7, 9, 10, 43
testicles 12, 47
testosterone 13
tobacco 19
'touching' activity 40
'tongue' activity 40

vaccinations 38, 43
vegetables 8, 9
viruses 16
vitamins 8, 9

water 9